1

I0482969

Should We Ignore The Reviewers
Versus Authors Wars?

The Degrading of the Publishing Industry

By: James M. Lowrance © 2014

2

TABLE OF HEADINGS:

(Total approximate word count: 7,180 Words)

HEADING ONE:

Is the Authors-Reviewers War Real or Imagined?

Some readers or browsers of my book titles, may be thinking to themselves that I'm in someway obsessed by the subject of the wars that go on between book reviewers and authors because I have several books published on the subject. I am not obsessed with the subject however (it is the least-covered among all my subjects), but I am obsessed somewhat with seeing the growth of the problem halted or at least quelled to a certain extent, for the sake of the publishing industry's future in general. At the same time, like most other Americans and people who live in other free countries, **I do want to see freedom of speech and expression preserved**. Can authors who feel their book(s) have been misrepresented as to their intended content, answer respectfully to those who may post those misrepresentations of them on their blogs, on forums or even at the location of book reviews for them? They should be able to do so in my opinion, <u>if they can leave out attacks</u> toward reviewers and not refuse to heed constructive criticism that could actually help them write better, more acceptable written works in the future. Can book reviewers show complete dissatisfaction for a book, without using abusive language toward a written work and without **attacking the author personally**. Again, yes they should be able to do so, without being made out as the villain for showing their dislike of books they have read.

4

The problem with both sides of the issue, is that each can seem to become highly offended at times or seem to believe they are above respectful reproach of any kind. If they can admit they may be wrong and allow their counterpart to say so, without flying off the handle and breaking out into wars over it, the world itself which is looking in on the behaviors of book reviewers and authors, will have <u>more respect for these venues</u>. Unfortunately, there is a very obvious element out there – a group pf people who literally **enjoy the degradation aspect** of trashing these venues and they are trying to accomplish it as an across-the-board attitude to be adapted over time, so that nothing within the two venues is sacred anymore so to speak. These are the people who you will hear telling others who are trying to retain some dignity within these venues, to *"grow the f**k up"*. Websites that allow reviews and reviews articles, are slowly allowing more of these type statements to stand and to remain as **permanent fixtures online**. Has it really come down to this?

Most readers of the question posed by this first heading, will say immediately to their selves "of course it's a real war that's going on between authors and book reviewers". The better question then I suppose would be as to whether or not the issues involved in the wars are really <u>worthy of addressing</u> to begin with? Especially with the fact that the "moderators" of these wars are beginning to no longer disallow comments.

5

I refer to comments that at one time resulted in website members being warned, penalized or in losing their memberships. Now, we have a more savvy population of online users, with the undesirable element among them **gaining an upper hand**, which has resulted in moderators and website administrators to give up on trying to stop the bad trends from growing. Members of sites who are reprimanded, can threaten to wage an online smear campaign against a site, they can find a way to hack them or to return and cause more problems under **multiple user-names**. Traffic and public confidence is very important to these sites and they each know that their actions in moderating members who join them, can be jeopardizing to their traffic and commerce. Each reader of this short subject book certainly has the right to disagree with me regarding the points I have made and that I will make following but **I do hope that most readers will make a serious consideration of them**. Some readers of this short subject resource, may rather believe that authors who are attacked, should not feel that it is wrong for those who are doing so or that reviewers who are attacked, should not feel that it is a wrong action by those perpetrators either. In reality, both parties should feel that the other involved party has a right to express her/his opinions about a book or a review but that **it should be done** "within reasonable decency". By this term, I simply refer to published opinions directed at other living people.

Those that contain attacks, defamation or purposeful twisting of what a book – or of what a review expresses generally (purposeful misrepresentation),via one's own public response to them.

I've made similar statements before but I will say again that "freedom of speech" has had its **definition expanded upon** by people who would like to see **an anything goes society** (at least they think they would). However, there are <u>laws</u> and online website <u>guidelines</u> that are supposed to prevent this from happening. They are not placed there to take away a free society but so that threats of murder, public rants or threats expressed otherwise, about a persons race, religion, sex or orientation, are all disallowed. By setting limitations on a freedom, you prevent chaos from evolving from it and you actually **protect many other rights** at the same time. For example, if one threatens someone else with bodily harm, publicly, this is an illegal expression that is not free to be practiced and can lead to the arrest of the guilty party. When you hear some proponents of **freedom of speech and expression**, defending that right (a very proper thing to do, when done in-balance), you would think that they believe these freedoms were granted to free societies, so that <u>anything can be said or expressed</u>. However, try expressing your perceived freedom to walk naked in a public place for example, and you are guaranteed to be thrown in jail or at least fined for either misdemeanor or felony "indecent exposure".

There have been blogs created addressing both sides of the "authors-reviewers wars" issue, being that of authors feeling that some reviews are going overboard by including attack type language within them. Some authors on the other hand, are not willing to receive **critical reviews of any kind**, even those that are written in a straightforward, honest fashion but that include some strongly-dissatisfied language within them (something I have been falsely accused of complaining about). Anyone... and I do mean "anyone", who does not see that there literally are two extremes that exist within the author and reviewer arena, either are **in purposeful denial** or they simply aren't paying attention. There are in fact authors who can't take even honestly-offered criticism and who actually attack reviewers for giving them an unfavorable review (I have never, nor will I ever attack a reviewer, regardless of my feelings about their intentions). There are in fact also reviewers who use reviewing as a type of leverage against targeted authors -- as a threat or an attack, rather than as an honest unfavorable evaluation of a book by them, that they've read.

I was somewhat drawn into this issue by a reviewer at Goodreads, who went through a number of my books and posted 5-star ratings on them. This was not requested by me and I did not know the person before finding these many favorable ratings. This was done after I published my first *experimental book* on the subject of "unfairly unfavorable reviews".

The member who gave me the many 5-star ratings, did so because they saw that my book on the reviewing subject, was received very unfavorably by some reviewers, while they agreed with the content of it. I am able to see every download of the eBook version and every purchase of the paperback version in my sales reports and the number of reviews that both the book and eBook versions received, was **at least 10 times the number of actual purchases/downloads**. The eBook was not in the sharing program by Amazon, where I published it exclusively, although I did offer it free for a short period, while monitoring downloads of it. It was also DMR protected (copy/paste disabled). This means that some reviewers based their evaluation on the book's description, exclusively. This is one of the types of responses I intended to gauge, while observing reactions to the book.

My feeling is that these reviews and/or ratings that have since grown to possibly 20 times the actual purchases of the book at the Goodreads website, were based simply on the fact that the subject was addressed at all (as evident in the book's description). I'm not sure these reviewers who evaluated the book based on what their reviewer-friends were saying about it (the only explanation for the number of reviews/ratings), realized or were made aware of the fact that **I have negative things to say about *some authors*, as much as I do about *some reviewers,*** within the content of the book.

This includes the fact that some authors resort to placing bad reviews on books they feel are competing with theirs (that's real desperation in operation). Authors also attack reviewers for unjustified reasons and they sometimes publish "trash books" (bad, insufficient content works) – an accusation that will likely be directed at me, regarding this book. I cover these facts in the first book I published on the author-reviewer wars subject as well.

I then followed up with this first experimental book and published 2 others that were written in comical/satirical, tongue-in-cheek fashion. **These were received very favorably**, I believe because they point out some of the ridiculous behaviors by authors and reviewers but behaviors that do not represent all participants in both fields. This in fact was the purpose of the funny versions, which I compiled together with the seriously written book, so that a reader can understand why these issues are being seen, some of which are real and others which are blown out of proportion and exaggerated. By the way, a disgruntled reviewer, saw the couple of dozen or so of my books that the well-intentioned book reviews member rated at 5-stars, and in turn, placed 1-star reviews on all of those same books, plus many others beyond that. I believe they did so because they felt it was an unfair advantage for the many 5-star ratings to be placed on my books at the Goodreads website, by another member there. I actually agree with their reason for adding the low ratings, although I'm not sure why they felt it necessary to post several dozen extra 1-star ratings.

In reality neither one of these actions hold much importance because it is obvious to other observers of this type activity, that **neither of the reviewers actually read the books they rated** (this is also why many customers pay no attention to star ratings).

Now to my point, reflected in the title of this short subject book, regarding why **I literally hate this "authors versus reviewers war"**. First, Amazon and other bookseller websites need to better moderate reviews (i.e. disallowing reviewers to swear at or resort to name calling toward authors and banning overboard, negative rants), all of which they encourage readers at their sites to help with by flagging them for moderators, when spotted on their site. And secondly, readers should be turning in authors who are disrespectfully responding to legitimate book reviews, there should be no issue on either side of the debate if these violating behaviors are **being given proper attention**. We live in broken world however, as my Christian faith recognizes and people are going to become offended at each other, when either valid or invalid problems are pointed out by either side of the debate. The bookseller sites know this. We then see a contest of wits that often follows, in which the two parties go after each other with attacks, including absolutely unnecessary, offensive language. This type of thing, in addition to highly inferior works being published by some authors, has degraded the publishing industry as a whole.

With some booksellers falling behind in removing both types of attack posts (those against reviewers and those against authors), the problem has potential to become far worse over time.

Would the best thing we can do, be to attack each other and to start mistrusting friends who you believe have turned against you (unjustified suspicion, which I assure you is happening) and to allow circles of gossip to also evolve? I would say with firm conviction, that **these things are the very root of this problem** and that the real answer is for those of us who see either authors or reviewers *behaving badly*, to be warned about it by "flagging them" when necessary. This is what the booksellers sites have placed those click-prompts on their sites for, that say to the effect *"Is this content improper/offensive?"*. Many people simply don't care and they will not flag attack posts of either kind. I personally have been guilty of this in the past and I have only reported offensive posts online, six times within the 10 years I have been online (as of this year 2014). Two of these were posts on a content-article site, not on a bookseller site and the other four were on bookseller websites (two were removed promptly).

I am determined however, to change this non-attentiveness on my part and to start flagging author and reviewer posts more often, that very definitely violate the Terms of Use (TOS) and guidelines of bookseller websites.

Will you join me in using this method of helping to control and to moderate offensive online posts that appear on these sites? While I realize we have "freedom of speech and of expression" in the USA for example, this privilege still has legal limitations placed on it. For example: you can't threaten someone, especially a politician and you cannot publish child porn. Yes, these are extreme examples among many others that could be cited but sometimes it's the only way some people will "get the point" regarding free speech, which **can very definitely be abused**. I have been told to "grow the f**k up" at times **by both authors and reviewers**, supposedly meaning that online posting has reached a new, more grown up level, in which we can all throw around as much offensive language and name calling as we like and *it's cool to do so*.

In reality this type statement is role-reversal (big time), a misnomer, a dichotomy and it is actually humorous when you think about how ironic it actually is. However, more statements of this type are stated by the age-groups who use reviewing as a game -- a contest in which you see how far you can go with statements you post online. Certainly all age groups have been guilty, however, Goodreads for example, allows people as young as age 13, to gain membership and to post on their site. This doesn't mean that all members of the site who are of this age-group, are irresponsible with their postings. **Most are very responsible** and even more so, than are some adults who post there.

13

With this said, I believe the age minimum should be a bit higher, such as age 16 or 18 required for membership. The maturity between teens, even when looking at age 13 versus 16, are quite significant.

I would really rather like to see publishing and reviewing venues, keep some quality-legitimacy in both authoring and book reviewing. I'm involved in both venues and I would implore readers of this short but hopefully well-expressed written work on the subject to join me, in keeping these venues as reasonably honorable pursuits, that's currently possible and for as long as we possibly can! While I do not believe this war will ever stop completely, I do believe that readers and authors who really care, can help to **quell the trend**, so that the "reviewers versus authors wars" do not permanently grow beyond the control of the reviewers-authors venues. The future of the literary world, literally depends on what we do now to save the future honor of them, for those who really care and who are not literally/literately playing games with them (trifling with venues that benefit many people)!

Thanks so much for your reading and your consideration on this very important subject, as we continue to the next headings.

HEADING TWO:

Integrity Eventually Always Wins Out... Always!

Some of the things I address and discuss in this chapter, may almost seem off-subject but I assure you, that they are very much on-subject and they represent examples of the same type of derision, attacks and well... **wars** that have developed between authors and book reviewers. Read on, to see what I mean by this. - - -

For several years, beginning in year 2003, I was given the position of moderator for several different fellow-patient support forums (mostly those for thyroid disease patients). Very few times over those years from 2003 to 2010, did I see truly heated arguments break out. When they did, I moderated them carefully and we always found peaceful resolution to strong debates that developed. It is a whole different animal when you're talking about exchanges between authors and reviewers because both sides can at times, feel that their freedom of speech and expression is being threatened. In many cases, both parties walk away from fights that develop, without them ever actually being resolved. Afterward, in many cases, the parties involved in online fights, will then launch online tirades against their perceived enemies, on blogs and at other forums, etc... In other words, they make it their purpose to trash their supposed enemies.

I involved myself in some online dogfights a few times, as simply a forum member in the past (forum debates that occurred over 5 years ago). Most of these involved the issue of **religious freedom** but very hateful, spiteful people came out of the woodwork, so to speak, when debates regarding "theism versus atheism" developed (belief and non-belief in God). How did any of these end? Well, every single one of them first grew into larger fights, with most of those who entered the fray, being the opposition to the side I was on. These were usually atheists who experienced terrible things in their lives, that turned them against belief in God. The protestors on my side of the debate, who were against attacks on their religion, kept their dignity purposefully because they knew the opposition wanted them to become the same type of undignified, online warmongers they were. The assaults by them, were as vile as it gets – take my word for it and these were designed to prove to believers, that they were just as vile as non-believers. In other words they wanted and did see some honorable people became dishonorable. In some cases believers did brake under pressure and began to attack their attackers but most refused to degrade their selves to this level. Everyone is capable of lashing out dishonorably, certainly myself included. Those who didn't, still hit walls/stalemates with the debates and this did nothing but make the opposition feel stronger and to push the envelope of indecency **just a little further, with each battle**.

I learned from this, that silence in the face of an attack, can be very frustrating to the one who is attacking you. The only way I can really explain what I have just said, is to give an example.

Several years ago, I was a member of an article-writers, content website. I wrote articles mostly on health but I also had a few on the site that were business subjects and others on short Christian Bible studies. I read on their religion forums very infrequently, mainly because it was mostly degraded type stuff being posted against Christians and yet it was a Christian discussion forum where most of these debates occurred. I saw where Atheists and Christians were **debating heatedly**. The main question from the Christian side, was as to why Atheists were constantly coming in and sabotaging their discussions with very vile posts. This eventually included them posting pictures of a gay Jesus, fooling around with his disciples, pictures implying Jesus was a child molester and launching direct attacks, including every expletive imaginable at Christian forum members.

At one point a lady on the forum made a very nice and convincing plea to me via a private message, asking that I help them to debate the anti-religion people (they were in most cases against "all religions" and they called believers "religionists"). I decided to go ahead and join the debate-discussions, making as many strong points for my side as I knew how to make.

The opposition I saw from this, was expected by me but when I saw that our protest against the ant-religion people, was only emboldening them even more to make horrendously vile statements against believers and **to blaspheme God**, I decided to leave the forum. I also took all of my articles off of the connected content website a few months later, as a protest against them not moderating vile forum posts and articles. The decision on the article removal was due to a man who claimed at one point to be a Satanist, actually writing anti-Christian articles, telling the Holy Spirit to "blank himself with a blank" (you can guess what was in the blanks). He had multiple user IDs, just as many people do on other social websites that lack proper moderation and one of his user-names was "UpHisAss", **a direct blaspheme toward God**, which included a pentagram with a goat head in the middle of it. The website eventually did have this member take down the offensive articles but it took them far too long to do so, in my opinion.

Through some search, I found that this guy was literally all over the place online. He's also highly educated and extremely intelligent. I found where he posed as a Christian on one of these and I took screen-shots of his avatars and showed them to a few people. This was when I first learned that IP addresses of PCs can be tracked to general locations, to determine if they are by the same person. They were amazed at how much posting this man was capable of accomplishing, on so many websites but they were creeped-out about it at the same time.

This man has made his way into almost every significant forum that exists, including an Amazon publisher's forum. He has also placed reviews on a couple of my books on Amazon that are each 5-stars, but he does a creep-out type review for them, consisting of masked insults, some readers will not see through. I have written Amazon only a couple of times over the years, about blatantly creepy reviews and they usually send me back emails saying "these reviews do not violate our guidelines". I recently read Amazon's newest guidelines for both reviews on their site and on Goodreads – their sister site.

They are holding back, soft-peddling in my opinion, regarding moderating vile reviews. They do say that they prefer reviewers do not attack authors directly but they state that if one does do this, they might say to the effect: *"This guy can't write a lick"*. Are they serious with these guidelines? It's difficult for me to even imply this much complaint on the issue regarding Amazon **because I'm grateful to them beyond measure** overall, for the many publishing venues they have given to me absolutely free! Hopefully it doesn't sound like I'm biting the hand that feeds me. I rather hope they see this as an attempt at constructive criticism because that is **exactly how I intend it**.

The backing off of reviews moderation, regardless of which bookseller we are talking about, is *the proverbial "inch", that will continue to be "taken a mile"*.

When the very bookseller sites themselves, are not going to prevent the vile stuff being posted or <u>will they only do so under extreme circumstances</u> to keep from offending customers, any debates regarding reviews, have then become a dead-end. I realize that sounds negative but you almost have to use an <u>indirect path</u> to bewilder your enemy at this point (total silence being one of those), especially when they have powerful backing. These short subject books are one of the ways in which I personally have expressed my concerns regarding **this war of dilemma** because only truly interested people are going to purchase them. I will find more ways to do this, as I go along. I have very strong debate skills – believe it or not but.... when I know my energies/strengths are being zapped by an enemy, while they tilt their heads back and laugh at the hamster on the wheel, I will not humor them. It's at points like these that after I have done all I can do within my own strength and in my own way, **I let God take over and fight my battles for me from there**. I can place <u>absolute faith</u> in the fact that he will do exactly that, regardless of who chooses to ridicule this statement! This type of talk doesn't scare non-believers -- which is not necessarily the point of them, in fact <u>they laugh at these type statements</u>. They have a surprise awaiting them however, because they will literally see God's defense of sincere people with integrity, in action, either sooner or later. **I am not holier, better or more loved by God than anyone else** but I am one of the people who care about where this issue is going.

What's my point to all this. Well as corny as it might sound there's an even better way that is seldom resorted to on the battlefield of book reviewers and authors. It's like the old Beatles song says, titled: *"We Can Work It Out"*, which says within the lyrics *"life is very short and there's no time for fussing and fighting my friends"*. I saw some of the Christian forum members I referred to earlier -- due to the multiple user-names held by some forum members, to actually start suspecting each other of being enemies in disguise! The out-of-control debates, bred confusion which the Bible says "Satan and not God, is the author of" (2 Corinthians 14:33). So these are the reasons, I am so reluctant to re-enter into debates of any kind online because it not only breeds confusion but it also brings about gossip and seriously hurt feelings, plus it places perpetrators in danger of reaping the same (Galatians 6:7). I have decided to express my opinions in the form of this short subject book because these can be read by interested parties and **I am not forcing these opinions on anyone**. My Christianity enters into it, simply because it is a part of everything I do in life and it is my freedom of religion, speech and expression.

It was important for me to say these things because if an ethical stance can be maintained on all levels and on every front, when it comes to trying to make a difference in **very real problems** -- vile book reviews and vile author responses to reviews being one of them, then I believe an actual difference can be made (sometimes a big difference).

With this said, I wish you who are sincere and honest in these venues, true success in your battle to see better moderation on book reviews and on authors who return attacks, against those who give them unfavorable reviews, whether they are honest ones or not. God will not defend this type of thing but he will defend debates that are launched honestly, rather than with the intent to hurt and to get revenge against people who begin an attack thread. Of course the attack type debaters would call this a **"holier than thou attitude"** or they will say that *"I'm a deluded Christian"* but this is not the case at all, regardless of weather they believe it is or not. They are certainly welcome to believe what they wish. I truly believe this point about taking an ethical stance, with absolute conviction and what seems to not be working, may be working better than we think. Such as removing ourselves from dead-end debates but flagging indecent posts or articles when necessary. It all depends on the power you have backing you up (sincerity or insincerity – honesty or dishonesty). Let me also add the point that there are social sites and adult sites, where posting expletive content is allowed, even between fellow forum members. In these cases, I respect the rights of people to say anything they want to each other. When a website is created/designed for these purposes, it is their prerogative and **I respect their rights to do so**. I also respect the rights of those who write and publish adult content romance novels and others with strong adult content.

If America says it's okay, then it's okay by rights and if a website says it's okay, then it's okay according to their Terms of Use and guidelines. How I believe these type things affect our society in these cases, then comes under the realm of my personal opinions and religious convictions, which I may express but that I will not force on anyone.

I'll end this heading by saying I appreciate readers of this resource, considering <u>my word offerings</u> – <u>my opinions</u> that have been sprinkled a bit with my Christian faith beliefs. I believe they are valid both with and without faith beliefs being expressed within them.

23

HEADING THREE:

My Previously-Written Works that Address This Problem from Other Angles

I saw where someone placed an unfavorable review for one of my recent *"Percyvelle Pennington III"* comedy audiobooks; one that is not on the authors or reviewers subject but that shows what I'm doing with this book-series character. Percyvelle is a pen name of mine that I use for directing some comedy at a few subjects of controversy and irritation, simply to lighten-up the subjects a bit, in attempt at showing readers that we don't have to take these subjects so seriously.

That is, unless they have truly gotten out of hand, at which time **inattentiveness can cause such a problem to implode**. Nose-blowing in the dining area of restaurants for example, is definitely not one of those serious problems and I addressed the issue purely for comedic purposes in one of my publications. It is an "irritation" not an actual issue in danger of imploding. This audiobook titled: *"Corrective Admonition for Restaurant Nose Blowers"*, can be accessed at Audible.com, Apple ITunes and is also available in Kindle eBook and in Paperback form.

I've been doing the publishing thing in books, since 2008 and I wrote online articles starting in 2004. I have seen this exact scenario before, in which someone received a "free download".

This was the case with the customer who downloaded the audiobook mentioned a moment ago -- which obviously means **they were not actually looking for outrageous comedy**. They chose the audiobook, "by accident" (uh huh, sure they did..... just kidding, no offense intended please). I think the production is hilarious and worth the price (especially at $3.95), but maybe I'm blinded by bias (or maybe Percyvelle is).

Think about it; you can buy a specialty coffee at Starbucks that costs more than $3.95, which is the price of the audiobook I have referred to and it will be drank within a few minutes. The funny Percy P. audiobooks and eBooks/paperbacks are obviously **meant for people seeking comedy** and they can be enjoyed more than once by a customer. I think the narrators did a great job with reading the book-manuscripts for the audiobooks, in a comedic fashion. In short, I believe the unfavorable review was probably written by someone who was using the review-opportunity as a chance to vent because they missed out on a jelly doughnut or for some other earth-shaking reason. They simply didn't understand the tongue-in-cheek, sarcastic, arrogant comedy. (Whoops! I think I'm speaking in Percy P. III mode, so I'll place my serious, real-self back to the front.) However, the review was not written offensively in the least although the reviewer expressed their displeasure for the audiobook, strongly yet without going on the attack. I appreciate this type of review.

Now to the next book I wish to point some discussion and description toward, titled: *"Effects of Unfairly Unfavorable Book Reviews on Independent Authors"*, which can be accessed in audiobook at Audible.com, Apple ITunes and it is also available in Kindle eBook and in Paperback form. Here I go, into a lengthy but needed description for this audiobook. I however, felt it was necessary to say a few things about this short written work, at **7,470** words in length because it has been mischaracterized by some people who have heard or read it. I will also talk about the two other books I have published on **"the authors and reviewers wars"** subject as well, following and how I also combined all three into a one-book resource. - - -

The most misunderstood point they make about the first book of the 3-part series (the one mentioned a moment ago), containing serious/sincere information, is that "I am an upset or *emo*/depressed author, because I received a bad review on my book" (as if I have only 1, instead of the 100 or so titles I actually have out). If they will use a little common sense, they will realize that I have been publishing written works online, since year 2004 and in book-form since 2008. I received bad reviews **long before I wrote this book** in year 2012, which is about "bad reviews that are not merited". In other words, it is about those reviews that are placed on books that in some cases, **misrepresent what they are actually about**.

This is the type misrepresentation the first book in this series has seen at times. In some cases a reviewer may have simply been in the mood to attack something, including the author, because they saw within a written work, something they don't like to see written about (and yet I'm characterized as the "whiny one" – a huge misnomer-reversal). The other possible scenario: A young person has gained membership on a social reviews website and is trashing books purposefully, **simply because he/she can.** It apparently gives them a rush -- a feeling of power, to play the game and to "one-up each other". I feel that the practice of <u>directly</u> abusing reviewers is **an equally bad practice** that authors <u>should not</u> engage in. My two comedy/satirical books on this subject, contain all fictional characters and **I make fun of authors as much as I do reviewers** within them (more information on these other two books, will follow).

I make it very clear in the serious book on reviews and authors, that 1-star reviews - in a scale of 1 to 5, **are not the problem** (star ratings don't mean diddly to most book shoppers) but rather the outlandish remarks that reviewers make within them, including <u>direct attacks toward authors</u> (name-calling, using swear words at them, etc...). The booksellers are just now starting to police these type reviews and Barnes and Noble has removed many of these type over the past few months (starting in late 2013 and this year of 2014). Amazon purchased the "Goodreads" social reviews media site last year.

They too have started to crack down on reviews practices, although it is such a huge undertaking that they are asking for members there and authors, who see highly unprofessional reviews-practices, to point those out to them. **Goodreads is a great site overall** and the bad elements there, are the exception and not the rule. Still 1,000s of pages there contain trash and Amazon has the power to remove it over time.

I ask again that **a little common sense be used** in realizing that you don't call authors **"a – h's"** or tell them to QUOTE: **"f 'ing grow up"** – a statement I have received, that's actually humorous because it's backwards, a role-reversal. And yet this and similar statements are found on Goodreads, stated literally 1,000s of times toward **both authors and fellow reviewers**. ADDED POINT: Some reviewers there have used terms to shelve books they've read into categories, such as **"d - head literature"** (an unnecessary expletive). Let's see if Amazon keeps these type terms on the site or takes them off, which will directly reflect on the Amazon company as a whole. My strong suspicion is that they will clean it all up over time -- it's definitely in their best interests to do so.

Some readers of the serious book, are or will be of the opinion that I'm trying to appear as *a martyr for fellow authors* and that *I'm sacrificing some of my own author reputation* for having written it.

The truth is however, that this is pretty much why I wrote it -- to demonstrate a need for moderation, over the importance of reputations or wrong opinions. I have addressed **many controversial/difficult subjects** in books over the years -- it's what I do, "it's my calling" so to speak, especially regarding controversial Christian and Bible subjects. I consider it a ministry. I stated on a publishers forum, long before the first book's release (the serious one), that it was going to be "an experiment of sorts". I saw fellow authors, both male and female who literally felt destroyed by "unfairly unfavorable reviews". I even referred to these type reviews as **"assassins bullets"** because these authors would post on publisher's forums, saying they would never write again because of unmerited attacks perpetrated on them via reviews. In most cases, reviewers are right in what they post and some authors really shouldn't be publishing until they gain better writing skills, while others who have **obvious, true potential** are attacked and completely discouraged. Authors **never reach perfection** but they can become acceptable and sometimes exceptional writers.

I would place a big bet on the fact that many of the type of overboard reviews containing expletives, extreme insults or excessive negativity, are written by very young people **who post attack reviews as sort of a game**, as previously stated or by some adults with very young/immature minds. I honestly do not believe some authors would be so highly discouraged by an unfavorable review that is written in an honest, critical fashion.

Those kind, that I have personally received in the past, did not discourage me but they rather inspired me to improve in the areas of my writing that reviewers may have complained about (whether a complaint was legitimate or not) but when posted in <u>an honest and straightforward fashion</u>.

I gave an example within the serious book in the series, of a review I received on a "health subject work" I published, in which the reader/reviewer perceived that I was against a particular treatment for the health disorder I address within it. Not only am I **not against the treatment in question**, that they misrepresented my intentions regarding but <u>I am actually highly pro</u> (for it), when it is overseen and administered by qualified doctors, rather than resorted-to as a "self treatment". It is dangerous and even life-threatening if administered incorrectly. I even cite medical studies about the treatment and how successful it has been **in people who are actually in need of it**.

Why did I cite this particular reader's review in the book (generally and not the specific review)? Because it was supposed to convey the fact that reviews, <u>in some cases</u>, **misrepresent what is contained within a written work**, as I also mentioned previously. I also state in the book, that in some cases reviews of these type are posted by **"competing authors"**.

These are authors who feel that by <u>degrading their competition</u> or at least their "perceived competitors", this will cause their own work in the particular genre they cover (the subject matter being addressed), to gain them an upward momentum in overall ratings, for their category.

I then continued "the experiment" by releasing two other books on the subject, in a tongue-in-cheek fashion, using a <u>comical approach</u> (I had fun with it) and I have received a series of 5-star, highly favorable ratings on these! The first comedy one being titled *"Writing Books that Won't Get Blue Meanie Reviews"*. You can go to the audiobook version link and **listen to a free sample,** at Audible.com or see it listed at Apple ITunes, Kindle eBooks and in Paperback form.

And the second comedy book on the subject is titled: *"Bashing Authors with Negative Reviews and Feeling Fully Justified"*. To see more on the audiobook version and to **listen to a free sample:** go to Audible.com or see it listed at Apple ITunes, Kindle eBooks and in Paperback form

The Blue Meanie Reviews book, has received a slew of positive 5-star and 4-star reviews, with only one truly unfavorable one. I say with absolute honesty that out of all the positive reviews it has received, I provided **<u>only two</u> of these reviewers** a free review copy of the book.

I do not know any of the other reviewers who praised the book and have never met them online or otherwise. I also compiled all three into one book (the serious one and the two satire ones together) and I received a lengthy, well-written, 5-star review on it as well, from someone I also do not know personally, online or otherwise. I titled it *"Wars Between Book Reviewers and Authors"*. Since I have the three in audiobook separately, I will keep the compiled one containing all three, in **Kindle eBook format only**.

Here's the point of the experiment and it's very simple: If you point out the "behaving badly" practices of people -- both authors and reviewers in a serious way, the work will likely be attacked by some readers. If you do so in a humorous, satirical way - without overboard trash language, people will understand your purpose-point and **they may receive the message of it more willingly**. In this way, you don't have to harp on negativity aspects, warring, arguments and other undesirable aspects, which the public has grown tired of hearing about. At the same time, we can't give up on making a difference regarding real problems that have potential to grow worse. What can I say? This has literally been the case with this experimental set of short subject books. {NOTE: I'm simply practicing "free speech" within the proper meaning of it in these books and not the **perverted meaning** (i.e. threats, personal obscenities toward others, defamation, etc...), wouldn't you agree?}.

Thanks again for reading my offered thoughts on this very difficult subject of wars between book reviewers and both legitimately and non-legitimately disgruntled authors. If I gain even slightly more attention from people who can make a difference in this war, it will have been well worth publishing this series of books on the subject.

(END)